The Gifting Boots
Tina Biby

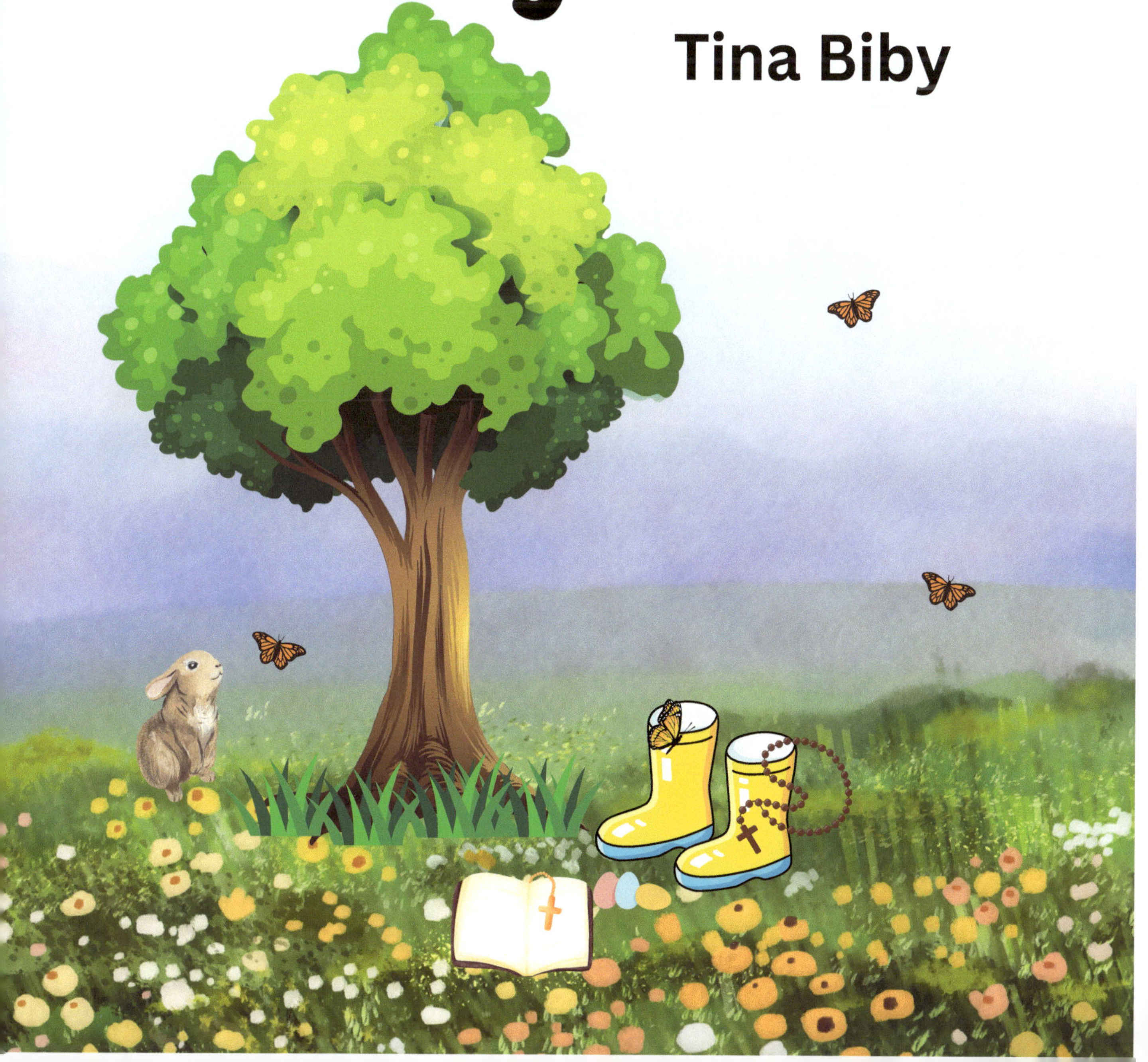

For Avery, McKinley, and Mya

ISBN 979-8-21863-387-5 (paperback)

Copyright © 2025 by Tina Biby

All rights reserved. No part of this publication may be reproduced, distributed, or transmitted in Any form or by any means, including photocopying, recording, or other electronic or mechanical Methods without the prior written permission of the author. For permission requests, solicit the Author via the email below.

Miss Tina's Book Mobile
Author Tina Biby
authortinabiby@gmail.com
authortinabiby.pubsitepro.com

Printed in the United States of America

Addy, Mattie, and Mya are cousins who live on the same street in their small town.
They are happy to have all their family around.
Today is Easter Sunday, a special family day.
After church, they are gathering at Grandma's.
She lives just up the way.

The girls were excited to visit Grandma today.
She always has a special gift and a story about Jesus
for every holiday.
As the girls ran through Grandma's back door and
into her kitchen,
They instantly smelled her delicious fried chicken!

They helped to set the table and the servings of food.
The girls waited to be seated so they were not rude.

Their family sat around the long table in prayer, Blessing Grandma's delicious meal they were preparing to share.

The girls excitedly ran into the room and sat on the floor.
Grandma picked up her Bible on the stand, next to the front door.

She picked up the gifts wrapped in a square box. Inside were rubber boots, and warm, fuzzy socks. The girls looked at each other and were excited to see which of their gifts were part of Grandma's Bible story.

11.

Inside the boots were toys of Jesus and the stable.
While Grandma read the Bible, they set each on the table.
Grandma read when Jesus grew up from a boy to a man.
He is the Son of God, who gathered followers to
Teach across the land.

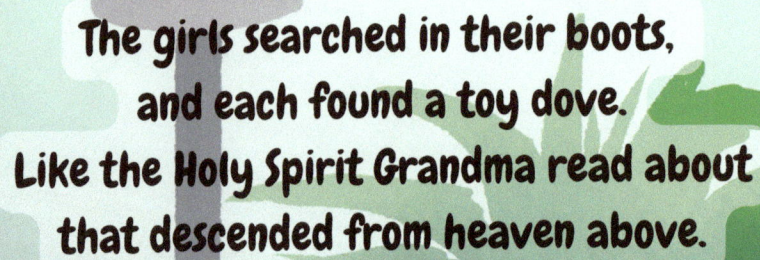

The girls searched in their boots,
and each found a toy dove.
Like the Holy Spirit Grandma read about
that descended from heaven above.

Grandma continued to read how Jesus rode a donkey into town.
And how the people came to greet him, placing clothes and branches on the ground.
The girls found a toy donkey and set it on the table, next to Mary, Joseph, and Jesus in the stable.

She read about Jesus speaking in parables, and how many people were healed.
They unwrapped small Bibles in boxes that were tied with ribbon and sealed.

26.

Grandma encouraged the girls to read
daily and learn God's word.
Inside are many stories of Jesus,
Our Savior, our Lord.
Jesus was crucified on the cross and
lifted for all to see.
He died for all our sins wholeheartedly.

The girls found another gift of a cross charm.
To remind them of Jesus' love and
his protection from harm.

JOSHUA 24:15

The girls know their Grandma loves them and cares.
With all the hugs, gifts, and stories of Jesus she shares.

Meet Chloe
THE PUG

About Me

Hi My name is Chloe and I am the little Pug dog in this story. My mom Tina loves to put me in her books. You can also find me in another book entitled, "Our Special Christmas Tree."

I am 15 years old and live on a farm in southern Illinois. I like to snuggle with our new kitten, Junior. Sometimes he snores and keeps me awake, but I don't mind. He likes to share my toys and my bed, too.

Did you know?

- I am on the front cover of this book.
- The girls in this book are my owner's grandchildren.
- The girls are jumping in a puddle on the cover and splashing water all over me!

What Am I Doing on the Following Pages?

- Page 7- With the broom?
- Page 11- What color is the bow on my head?
- Page 14- What am I chewing?
- Page 15- What am I reaching for?
- Page 17- What is on my head?

What do you notice?

Look on Page 3- What am I doing? (I am jumping on Mya.) Do you think I was happy to see her? Yes!
Look on Page 4- That is Junior, what is he doing?
Look on Page 5- What do you think I am waiting on? I smell food and I am always hungry.

I Love My Family!

Page 19- What am I trying to do?
Page 21- What color is the egg I am trying to play with?
Disscus what I am doing on pages 23, 26, 28, 29, and 32.
Most importantly I love my family!

MEET THE Author

About Me

I am a Christian, Mom, and Grandma. I love to work with children and read and write children's books.

Hey! I am Tina Biby

I am the author of this and many other children's books! Check out my website for a list of my books.

Contact Details:

You can find my books anywhere books are sold.
You can contact me via email at authortinabiby@gmail.com
Online- authortinabiby.pubsitepro.com

I believe that curiosity is the driving force behind meaningful learning. As an author and teacher, I aim to spark your curiosity about the natural world and instill a sense of wonder about the world around us, all while learning new things.
God Bless and thank you for reading my book!

www.ingramcontent.com/pod-product-compliance
Lightning Source LLC
LaVergne TN
LVHW071659060526
838201LV00037B/384